Fragrances of Old Cathay

A Scot, Gordon Wallace was born in Renfrew in 1931 and schooled in Paisley. He read English and History at Glasgow University. Following National Service in Malaya he spent five years in Northern Nigeria, ending up as a District Officer before returning to Oxford University to read Geography. He married, had his two sons of whom he remains proud and fond, and taught in Dover Boys' Grammar School. He served with the British Council in Nairobi and from 1966 to 1980 he was a member of HM Diplomatic Service, serving in London, Laos and Singapore. His last ten years of active service were spent teaching in a comprehensive school in Oxford. His wife died of Alzheimer's in 2004. He learned his (limited) Chinese in retirement. His sons are both married and each has one child.

Fragrances of Old Cathay

distilled from the writings of leading poets of Imperial China

Gordon Wallace

JON CARPENTER

Acknowledgements

Publications

Only one of these poems has previously been published, about three years ago in the *Oxford Magazine*, to the Editors of which I am grateful for publishing it in the first place and for raising no objection to my reprinting it here.

Thanks

I should like to thank Olivia Byard and members of her poetry workshops at Ewert House, Oxford, for guidance during my poetic apprenticeship; also my 'Isis Poets' colleagues for their constructive and judicious consideration over the last year or two – to the considerable improvement of several of the poems here. Most of all I am grateful to Bernard O'Donoghue who read virtually all of these poems several years ago when they were still in embryonic state, and who gave me the encouragement and the courage to persist in my endeavours.

First published in 2007 by Jon Carpenter Publishing
Alder House, Market Street, Charlbury, Oxfordshire OX7 3PH

The right of Gordon Wallace to be identified as author of this work has been asserted in accordance with the Copyright, Design and Patents Act 1988

All rights reserved. No part of this publication may be reproduced, stored in a retrieval system or transmitted in any form or by any means electronic, mechanical, photocopying or otherwise without the prior permission in writing of the publisher

© Gordon Wallace

Our books may be ordered from bookshops or (post free) from Evenlode Books, Market Street, Charlbury OX7 3PH.
Phone 01608 811969   E-mail: orders@joncarpenter.co.uk
Credit card orders should be phoned or faxed to 01689 870437 or 01608 811969

ISBN-10 0-9549727-9-1   ISBN-13 978-0-9549727-9-0

Manufactured in the UK by LPPS Ltd, Wellingborough NN8 3PJ

Belatedly, for Jade

Shelley

With kind & affectionate regards.

Gardner

May 2008

Foreword

The originals of most of the poems that follow were written by poets who lived during the Tang Dynasty, AD618-907, the golden age of Chinese Poetry. Where the original poems are much earlier than this, indicative dates are given. A few of the poems are from later Song and Ming times, 10th to 15th Century, but these and the Tang Dynasty poems are not separately dated.

The 130-odd poems presented here have been selected from New Poems From Old Cathay, a rather more comprehensive collection than this, with detailed notes and appendices. As yet the larger collection awaits a publisher.

In making my translations I have in almost every case worked from the Chinese originals first before checking my renderings against such published translations as I have been able to locate (and understand) in English, French, or German. A short note on whether and to what extent early Chinese poetry can be translated – if indeed it can be translated at all – may be found at the end of this collection.

Traditional Chinese poetry was written primarily for court circles. It is under-stated, urbane, orderly, well crafted and well mannered, even when expressing strong emotion. I have tried in my translations to convey something of this under-stated orderliness while sacrificing as little as possible of the original wording. But, as a Chinese philosopher once indicated, when busy catching a fish it is sometimes necessary to concentrate on the fish without fussing too much about the reticulation of the net.

GW

Table of Contents

Childhood, Youth, and Courtship	9 – 13
Marriage and Family Life	14 – 19
Friendships and Farewells	20 – 23
Old Age	24 – 27
Waters and Hills	28 – 31
Birds and Beasts	32 – 33
Flowers and Gardens	34 – 35
The Four Seasons	36 – 39
Festivals and Entertainments	40 – 43
Wine, Women, and Song	44 – 47
The Lot of Palace Maids	48 – 51
The Labouring Poor	52 – 55
Public Office, Retirement, and Exile	56 – 61
Travel and Adventure	62 – 65
War and its Woes	66 – 73
Life, Dreams, and Afterlife	74 – 78
Translator's Note, and Chen Zi'ang Poem	80 – 81

Bemoaning my Sons

Tao Yuanming AD365-427

I'm white-haired now
thin as a rake.
My five young sons
just will not take
to brush or book.

A-shu, sixteen
lies in till ten;
A-xuan, fifteen
has never seen
the need of pen.

Then Yung, and Tuan
both thirteen years
could not add six
to seven pears
lined up for them.

Dong-zi is nine
and does he shine?
At climbing trees.

They just don't please –

I'll stick to wine.

Supercilious Youth

Du Fu

Well mounted, self-possessed. *How white his face!*
Whose son is this young lord?
He casually dismounts, takes someone's place
deigns not a single word
says nothing of his name nor where he's from
the supercilious turd.
His languid nail selects the silver urn
to say, *Well, get it poured!*

Silks and Gold

Du Qiunniang

Don't squander youth pursuing silks and gold
when perishable dainties hint at feasts.
It's spring, your chance to help sweet buds unfold,
dull autumn's blooms mere desiccated dust.

Perfumed Maidens

Li Xun

The gaily painted skiff
glides round the lotus pool.
The ducks, in pairs, are startled
when some girls start to sing –
while laughing girls, in garlands, clasp friends or ask in fun
Am I the prettiest one?
huge lotus leaves their parasols against late slanting sun.

Love-lorn

Wen Tingyun

Bright sunshine gilds silk screens that keep her fair,
white cheek caressed by scented raven hair.

Awake at last she washes, finds a comb.
She's slow with make-up, pencils eyebrows thin
as moth's antennae. Bronze mirrors aid her art,
embroidered birds in every silken part.

She smoothes a golden partridge, tries to catch
the image and the silk until they match –
pleased to find her love bird one of a pair.

Be Modest, Sir

From The Shijing Collection c.600BC

Pray keep your distance, sir
and don't presume too far.
Don't break our willow tree!
That might not worry me
but parents' wrath soon would.
Do I like you? Well I may
but I mind what parents say.
Please do only what you should.

Pray, please don't take me ill
but you mustn't vault our wall
or snap our mulberry tree
in paying court to me.
My brothers would take on
and, like you as I may,
just think what they would say.
I know you should be gone.

No! Don't come on our land,
and presume to hold my hand.
Please watch that myrtle tree
if you must pay court to me.
What will the neighbours say?
I'll love you if I may
but leave me now, I pray
else they'll go on all day.

Spring Promenade
Wei Zhuang

Spring.
Adrift on the air
apricot petals catch in my hair.

How distinguished that gorgeous young man
   by the path. Whatever's his name?
I really must have him for mine,
   quite glad to be principal wife
   for the rest of my life.
Even if later displaced
I'll not feel disgraced.

Lamenting a Prize Bloom
Du Mu

Judge of prize blooms, forestalled of primacy
I can't begrudge the blush you take from time.
Gales may have torn some blood red petals off
but swelling fulness hints at fruits to come.

Village Near the River

Du Fu

The river wraps us round, flows crystal clear
all summer long. Our life here is serene.
Two swallows come and go – always a pair –
whole family groups of seagulls skim, or preen.
My wife is ruling squares for playing jí,
our sons are beating fish-hooks from some pins.
I'm poorly, search for leaves to brew herb tea
but that apart I'm happy to stay home.

Saying Goodbye to My Daughter

Wei Yingwu

My stomach tied in knots, the days drag on.
I come and go, divorced from what and when.
My daughter's pledged to cross that one-way stream –
what bridal boat has ever brought girls home?

Embracing new-found kin one's heart rebels
but still, she may yet find a mother's love.
Her sister brought her up and their farewells
bring double tears. Well, fondness may yet grow;
that thought must help console our aching hearts.
Keep her here unwed? No way for her to go.

Yet there was none to guide her in her youth. I fear
that she may fret at guidance now.

> *We know you're going to a gentle home,*
> *they're decent, feeling people, won't impose.*
>
> *Meet need with thrift, remain sincere;*
> *as dowry, take no goods but your good sense.*
> *Respect your elders as becomes young wives*
> *eschew all double dealing and pretence.*
>
> *This morning here we needs must say goodbye,*
> *who knows how many autumns till we meet?*

I've always held emotions well in check
but feelings sadly sap declining years.
Returning to our home, her sister's sad,
I find my cap-strings wet with hidden tears.

Farewell

Du Mu

Deep feelings hide within, allow the face no part.
We sit, our cups in hand, with outward show of calm.
But parting's heavy grief. Wax candles act our heart
by shedding burning tears until long after dawn.

River Trader

Li Bai

A Ballad from Zhongkan

Young playmates: I an opera star
with snapped-off flowers in page-boy hair
while you rode bamboo horses, dear.

Young sweethearts: we'd play round the wells
in Zhongkan, casting greengage spells
untroubled yet by all life's ills.

At fourteen I became your bride
so bashful that I nearly died,
dared not look up, tongue humbly tied.
You called, my Lord, and I would hide.

Fifteen. I longed to be with you
inseparably one, we two;
swore, come what may, that I'd be true –
could I need look-out tower for you?

I rose sixteen. You would not stay.
In June you sailed, too late they say,
for Qutang Gorge where rocks stalk prey
and apes' cries echo night and day.

I see still where your feet have been,
the prints grow moss as days draw in.
I have no heart to sweep them clean
nor autumn leaves, blown here too soon.

September, in the evening air
the butterflies flit pair by pair.
Can you not feel my long despair,
sense wearying face that waits you here?

Once you know when you'll leave San-pa
please let me know, I'll leave that hour
to meet you – I won't think it far.
Let's meet at Long Wind Sands, my dear.

Since You Left

Zhang Jiuling

Since you left, my only love,
I pick at things, do nothing right.
My lord, unlike the moon above
I die a little more each night.

Loving Husband

From the Shijing Collection c. 600BC

There's a girl, in silks like clouds,
by the East-Gate, one of a kind.
But even were there crowds
they would soon slip from my mind.
In plain white silk, blue shawl,
my wife's my very all.

When you leave by the turret gate
slim as thistles, girls entránce,
adorned as in robes of state;
but they do not hold my glance.
Only one holds me in thrall:
in madder rags she'd be my all.

Irreplaceable Mother

Meng Jiao

This loving mother just won't tack
the shirt on her rapscallion's back.
She stitches closely, neat and strong,
sound judge of filial 'Won't be long'.
What cutting, thriving in the spring
could pay the sun its reckoning?

Chaste Wife

Zhang Ji

You knew, Sir, I was wed
yet sent two shining pearls.
I'm touched, almost misled,
might hide them in silks and veils.

He's given me courts and gardens for his part;
my husband's just and held in high esteem.
I know that what you did came from the heart
but marriage binds; I cannot share your dream.
I send back your two pearls, my tears inlaid,
so sad we did not meet when I was maid.

Unexpected In-Laws

Du Fu

In spring it's really wet all round our plot
though gulls enjoy that – some come every day.
Our floral path's not fit for city foot
let's use the wicket gate, I've swept the way.
The market's far, our food is dull and bland;
poor wine, lees-rich, is all we've ever got.
I'll call across the hedge if you don't mind;
my neighbour won't mind lees, he'll help with that.

Visiting an Old Friend at his Smallholding
Meng Haoran

My dear old friend has really done me proud
with chicken-millet in his homely yard.
Green trees half mask his home from winds and chills
that leap town walls and sweep down from the hills.
From bamboo mats we view his kitchen plot,
we nurse our drinks, we talk of this and that.
I must come back! Chóngyáng, the best of times,
the Double Ninth, for the chrysanthemums.

Misjudged Visit to a Friend's Garden
Ye Shaoweng

I've marked the moss! Ashamed my footprints cling
I call, but gently. No one hears my calls.
Shut gates shield blooms but can't impound the spring.
Bright sprigs of blushing almond out-top walls.

Meeting an Old Acquaintance in a Distant Town
Wang Wei

A fellow townsman. You've just come?
Tell me your news – I can hardly wait.
You know, by my curtained window frame,
is my winter plum in blossom yet?

The Clearing Winds of Autumn
Zhang Ji

In Luoyang an autumn wind clears mists. Now I can see
the things my letter fails to say; I'm troubled in my mind.
I've countless thoughts, could fill a book explaining all I feel.
The courier waits, and now just look
I've gone and spoiled the seal!

Meeting a Courier on his Way to the Capital
Cen Shen

Friend's farm. The road leads east. But home's a distant land.
My sleeves are now in tatters, they dry my tears at best.

Tell them we met a-horse, no writing things to hand;
just find a form of words to set their minds at rest.

A Promise of Spring
Huang Yungwu

I'll snap a plum branch when the courier calls
for something to send to the people back home.
There's nothing down south here to send folks at all,
the best I can manage, a promise of spring.

A Chance Meeting
Dai Shulun

The season autumn, the moon again full. Close by the
city gate tower, as on any of a thousand
nights, still thinking you have gone back south I
see you. Am I dreaming? Is it really you?

A gust in the branches startles the dusky
magpies and bends dew-laden grass to discomfit
small things there. We who travel by horse do well
to drink at length. All dread the parting at dawn.

Farewell
Li Bai

Hard on the town's north wall lie cold blue hills;
here, east of town, white waters carve their course.

This is the place to take our brief farewells –
then drift like tumbleweed, for months a-horse,
minds fancy-free as clouds upon the breeze
each sinking sun recalling friendship here.

Let's bow, each clasp his hands, then simply leave.
Unharnessed, we'll hear whinnying from afar.

With Heavy Heart

Meng Haoran

Neglecting even hills, the sun goes down.
Out east the moon moves slowly on the lake.

Hair loose, to catch the cooling evening air
I open up the house, tall bedroom doors.
A fragrant breath of lotus scents the breeze;
dews, dripping from bamboos, surprise the ear.

I strum at strings in search of soothing chords
but can't evoke the solace that I seek.

My heart is choked with thoughts of absent friends,
my nights of longing filled with careworn dreams.

Farewell from the Hills

Wang Wei

Hills lock me in now friends have gone.
Dusk shrouds the kindling by my door.
Green springs, we know, will come again.
Will friends I treasure come once more?

Song by Lake Qiu

Li Bai

Around Lake Qiu, a mile or so
first tresses of the winter's snow
– would sorrows were no longer!
The waters mirror snow that's there
but mirrors leave me wondering where
I've gained the hoar-frost in my hair.

Crossing the Han River

Li Pin

Across those hills no tidings ever came
but winters came, in turn replaced by springs.
As home draws near my heart now slows my feet;
I dare not even question those I meet.

Returning Home at Last

He Zhizhang

I left here as a youth, come back as an old man.
My hair has mostly gone but still I've kept my tongue.
The children comprehend me but don't know who I am
and laughingly they ask me: 'What place do you call
  home?'

Recruited at Fifteen

From the Collection of Ballad Songs of the Bureau of Music, Han Dynasty (c.120-6BC)

Recruited at fifteen for foreign wars,
discharged at eighty, lucky to return.
A chance encounter with a local man
who took me by some ways I'd not have known
and pointed out the place that was my home –

home now to cypress; thickets, too, of pine;
a warren, where dogs chase and rabbits run.
Now on my roof-trees pheasants make their home,
within my yard grow patches of wild grain
while mallows by the well thrive in the sun.

I'll grind some grain to make a little gruel
prepare some mallow soup,
that won't take long.
Except – why need I cook them, and for whom?

Now looking back to where today's sun rose
I just can't staunch the tears that damp my clothes.

The Plateau of Loyou

Li Shangyin

The days draw on. Cares weigh when one
must slowly climb to these high plains
where sallow dusk waits each alone.
Yet worlds glow gold in setting suns.

Yangzi and Han

Du Fu

Well known around Yangzi and Han,
this broken old scholarly man.

White clouds drift off through the blue.
In the night, a bright moon passes through.
Suns set, but there's warmth in them still.
Autumns chill, but he claims he's not ill.

We usually put hacks out to grass.
Just let him be. He'll soon pass.

Taking Leave of a Grandson
Yuan Zhen

Years pass, and slowly filch our ageing kin.

One tear-smirched elder, blessing a grandson:
Death's dart is sure, I've known that all along,
this body's done, it's time I took it home.

Elderly Member of the Imperial Academy
Yuan Zhen

Clustered under eaves –
dried fish-scale look-alikes?
swept leaves: spent, green; one yellow from the frost?
– some aged men; a skilled musician.

Death waits until he's played. But now he's lost.

Boyang (South Lake) and Lushan (Hill-Station Mountain)

Zhan Fangsheng, fl. c. AD400

Three tribute-bearers keep lake coffers charged
transmuting sands to silver in clear streams.
Above kow-towing foothills Lu looms large.
Tall pines, dark acolytes, robe crags in greens.

How long since waters learned to run
since hills and trees encompassed them?

Unchanged, great hills and streams remain.
Men pass, give way to other men –
mere motes amidst a vastness of infinities,
our *was* and *is* mere fragments of eternities.

City of Stones

Liu Yuxi

Encircling hills stand firm, Old Kingdom walls in ruin.
Tides lap the soul-reft town, in silence ebb forlorn.

East of the River Huai moons gently bathe the night.
Here? storm stark battlements with shafts of light.

Benighted on the Jiande River
Meng Haoran

Still at risk on river. Bare isle, no berth, too clouded.
Shelter offering never; moorings mist-enshrouded.
Dark and fear encroaching; sun and light now fleeting;
stark moon, afloat, approaching – pellucid stream
   entreating.

Autumn Evening on Dongting, the Great Lake
Wang Changling

Afloat, at night. Thin mist. Sparse rain strikes chill
but on Dongting there's hardly any frost.
The moon clears, swings in time with swaying boat,
the night so still. Like souls from sleepers' dreams,
breaching the breath of air that herds the mists,
the sudden honking of a skein of geese.

Wishes
Pei Di

Lay hold on each fold of these hills,
every beauty of form and of line.

Ours to call up from dreams when we will?
Ours to see now and no other time?

In Reply to His Majesty
Tao Hungjing

Hills, Sire asks. *What's found up there?*
Bare ridges; many clouds, harmonious, white;
enough to pleasure such a one as I
but nothing one can bring to noble lords.

Why Hills?
Li Bai

You perch in grass-green hills! And why so choose?
My beard just masks my smile. I'm calm, serene.
Peach blossom, babbling brooks, mysterious views –
that is my world: complete, untouched by man.

Mount Tong
Li Bai

To plumb the joys found at mount Tong
a thousand years were none too long.
I'd need my dancing sleeves until
I'd partnered every maid on Five Pine Hill.

Spring Torrents
Wang Wei

At rest. Osmanthus flowers fall.
Spring evening, hill, deserted scene.
At moon-rise hill birds call and call.
The torrent's drowned in its ravine.

Watching the Waterfall at Lushan
Li Bai

The sun strips purple mists from Censer Peak.
   From far the waterfall
   becomes a floating veil.
Three thousand feet of waters float and fly –
a Milky Way. Our ladder to the sky?

In the Mountains
Wang Wei

In Bramble Burn
white rocks return;
cold skies, a few red leaves.
On mountain path
just withered heath,
blue void where clothing cleaves.

Wild Swan

Zhang Jiuling

Lone swan from the sea, catching sight of a pond
does not dare to set down. Banking round, without sound
he spies emerald birds nesting high above ground
in a poplar's pearl shade.

This perch that you've found,
is it treasure to trust? Aren't there people around,
even slingshots to fear? Fine plumage is grand,
don't men covet your plumes? Those who flaunt, risk deep
  wounds,
may pay more than pride's worth. Whereas I move around
in the dusk or the dark. Has the dart yet been found
that will bring me to earth?

Cormorant Creek

Wang Wei

He skims red lotus – *There he dives!*
All sparkling, surging from the creek,
the poseur preens as he arrives
on floating log, a fish in beak.

Ferghana's Fame

Du Fu

Barbarian renowned, Ferghana's Fame
sharp-featured, horse of lean and wiry frame:
a bamboo tuft each sharp upstanding ear
quick dainty feet that whistle through the air.
Wherever next, however far, you've breath,
sure-footed, where sure foot means life from death.

O quadruped divine, why, given the plain
you'd race a thousand leagues and back again.

White Deer

Zhi Jianwu

Snuffling in crevices, worrying out buds in the dark.
Two worlds, two closed books, what basis for either to
   judge?

You're not just a snowy white pelt or guttural bark

you vandal!
you've trampled young peach trees to cross the stone bridge.

Thoughts

Zhang Jiuling

Spring orchids can cascade like ramping knotweed
while autumn showers bright cassia-barks with flower.
Plants find, in season, reason for display
occasions for their festivals of blooms.

Who knows? Might creeping things that scour the
   woods
delight to sniff sweet scents that charge the air?
Could shrub or tree – they must at root have hearts –
forgive even gorgeous girls who cull their flowers?

Golden Valley Garden

Du Mu

In summer shimmering blooms
by autumn fragrant dust;
did brooks delight in spring to help them slake their
   thirst?

East winds arrive with dusk;
birds sulk, draw testy breath.
Like favourites, petals fall. Can charm cheat early death?

from Flowers by the River
Du Fu

   I
These quilts of stream-side flowers inflame the brain.
Who can I tell? I totter round to claim
assent from bosom pal in neighbouring plot.
He's ten days gone, bed empty. Drunken sot!

   II
Our hearts go out
to flowers –
   such beauty
   courting death.

A brave parade –
   buds burst
   blooms fade
   boughs fall.

Should we then sigh
   as new leaves vie
   to paint the sky?

Spring Suns
Li Shangyin

Spring suns just hug horizons, never high.
A nightingale will tantalise then fly.
The transience of it pains,
starts tears to rival rains

Spring Winds
Du Fu

Don't imagine, come spring, that all's well.
Crazy winds rage, quite out of control
dashing blossoms to earth-spattered pools,
broaching fishermen's skiffs in wild squalls.

Who's Spring gone off with?
Huang Tingjian

Who's Spring gone off with?
  She left on her own.
If anyone sees her
we want her back soon.
Who'd know how to trace her?
  Spring birds would have known.
Who'd know where to find them?
  Spring Flowers, but they've blown.

Summer Procrastinates

Yuan Zhen

The months can't wait but summer won't be rushed:
    thin layers of cloud won't cluster into towers,
    the ground's still softly draped in rosy blush,
    high up, no billowing crests, just whitish haze.
Yet who would squander fertilising showers
on too impatient soil? One hoarding seed
hears all too clearly, craving brief surcease,
insidious dragons whisper   *Now!*   *Release!*

Fisherman's Song

Zhang Zhihe

From here to West Fort Hill white herons dare to fly.
Peach blossoms strew the stream, the perch look nicely
    grown.
    For hats, bamboos braid sky
      green leaves weave coats, dare I
not brave light breeze, fine rain? Who needs to rush
    back home?

Harbingers of Change

Du Fu

As rivers turn to jade some birds turn pale.
As flowers start to fade the hills, unveiled,
mature to greens that will not re-appear
when spring brings fresh new greens to start the year.

Early Autumn

Xu Hun

Unseen, afar, soft lutes have charmed mild nights.

Now, west winds bring fresh vine-scents on cool airs.
Tonight then, dews will quench our fireflies' lights
and early geese eclipse bright shimmering stars.
By dawn all will be clear – trees: great dense stands
beneath wide skies; far hills: one long gold crest.

In Anhui one leaf falls and summer ends.
Time there creeps gently on in swirls of mist.

Autumn Flood at Báidì Gorge

Du Fu

On the hill squalls drive down scorning door, drenching home;
on the plain it's as wet as if baths had upset.
Towering floods in the gorge – lightnings thunder and scourge.
Spray-soaked, in deep gloom vines blot out sun and moon;
racing streams in steep courses outrun charging horses.

Where a hundred homes stand a full thousand are drowned.
A few women call, implore death to end all.
Is no part of our plain free from weeping and pain?

Winter Hunt

Wang Wei

Keen winds shirr taut strings on horn bows:
our General hunts in full flight.
Coarse tussocks lie threatening in snows
but eagle-eyed hunters tread light.
Ignoring lush market's appeal
we course through sparse willows again
seeking out what the vultures revealed
when they stooped in dark clouds to the plain.

Mountain Excursion

Du Mu

The higher the colder:
paths wander and twist above homes still in mist.
Mist clears. *Stop the carriage!* I adore maple bowers,
the leaves frosted red – precocious spring flowers

Snow on the River

Liu Zongyuan

A thousand hills: not one bird, high or low.
Ten thousand paths where no one dares to go.
Now gathering snow: one skiff, straw cape, leaf hat –
an old man hoping fish will take his bait.

The Day of the Spring Sacrifice
Wang Jia

Chinese New Year

Around Goose Lake: rice paddies, millet land,
half-open gates half guarding coop and pen.
White mulberries, long shade. Feast at an end,
drunks propped by dozing drunks returning home.

Double Ninth Day
Li Bai

Soft sunlight's pastel tints fade from calm clouds;
green waters darken, dusk invades my hills.
On rosy wine, now ruby, petals float –
chrysanthemum, in honour of the day.

Long vistas, ancient pines, dark age-old rocks;
borne on the wind, music of strings and flute.

Glimpsed in the cup, my solitary face
dimly carousing here, all on my own
my hat fallen off, drunk amidst moonlit hills.

I sing of friendship
from an empty heart.

Qingming Festival

Du Mu

The Clear and Bright Day
when the graves of ancestors are swept.

Qingming. Graves still unswept as rain pours down,
the roads still full of people – out of heart.
What else but ask for wineshops? Yonder town?
   The herdboy's nail points out
   afar, a flowering apricot.

Cold Food Festival

Han Hong

For Cold Food Festival the weather's fair:
throughout the town, spring blossom everywhere –

blown by east winds that make royal willows lean,
that tear at wisps of mist and shred the air
toward dusk, till candles set by palace men
disperse the gloom invading Five Dukes' Hall.

Sword Dance

Du Fu

Long years ago a matchless dancer, *Elder Sister*, a Gongsun girl
set the whole far west ablaze.
People stared in droves, amazed, struck pale as at a funeral.

Her sword dance brought the heavens to earth, translated earth aloft:
a god on dragon wings to match the hero archer who dispatched
unwanted suns with nine true shafts.

When she advanced the lightning raged, and when she stood
four seas would freeze, their sparkling radiance locked.

Long gone her crimson lips, brocaded sleeves.

Now a newcomer's dancing thrills, recalling fragrance hoarded long:
a beauty from Linying, graceful, gracious, strong,
commanding at her lightest whim: lissom, imperious, challenging.

So Elder Sister's art, thought lost, now seems at last
to have been passed intact to one of worth.

One still regrets eight thousand ladies who would vie
to catch the Emperor's kindly glance, compete to meet
some mild request while Gongsun danced her famous
    dance,
the foremost and the best.

So fade some fifty years in the gesture of a hand.

Now wind-blown dust accumulates around decaying palace
    gates,
the Royal Players long dispersed like mist.

Only remains, in memory's eyes, a dancing girl, a bird in
    flight
incomparable, beyond praise, radiant in the cool sunlight
where *Golden Millet Tomb* now lies, hidden in a grove of
    trees.

Grasses now seek foothold there, on the walls of Qutang,
    where
no lutes of tortoise-shell sustain last lingering long-drawn
    chords.

Our pleasures soon expire, and griefs soon settle in
to grow like waxing moons, till one old man at last
no longer knows whether he comes or goes,
lurching through barren hills; alone, in pain,
all too constrained to take his time.

Drinking Alone in the Moonlight
Li Bai

What better amidst flowers than flasks of wine?
Yet I'll not drink alone, friends need their friends.
Suppose I toast friend Moon? He'll surely shine
then with friend Shadow we'll be three. Three's fine.

Old Moon's not used to drink and does not sing
and Shadow, while he mimics only mimes
but I shall drink to both; they'll have their fling.
Time's short, besides, and joys die with the Spring.

For lighting up night's skies I'll sing Moon's charms;
I'll dance, dear Shadow clasped in ample arms
and, sober, we'll commune till dawn alarms.

Then drunk, we'll each seek out a separate way
nor think to pledge our hearts. Yet, come what may,
amidst the stars we may just meet one day.

Drinking with a Recluse in the Mountains

Li Bai

We two have measured out the wine
in time with hill-flowers' openings –
a cup, a cup, a cup again.

> *I'm tired; you're drunk; hie you off home.*
> *Tomorrow, should you chance along,*
> *bring lutes. We'll try the power of song.*

Chrysanthemums

Wei Yingwu

In Imitation of Tao Yuanming

When frosts and dews have struck down shrub and
    flower
chrysanthemums alone shine fresh and fair,
immutability their hidden power
immune to winter's blast or summer's glare.

Their petals shimmer on our cloudy wine:
sundown; your farm; we share things as one should
and drink like very sots beneath the eaves.

What virtue in unstinted plenitude.

Benighted Homecoming
Du Fu

Home heaves in view by mid-of night. The tiger-gauntlet's run.
A mound of darkness, all wrapped tight, they're sound asleep at home.
The Bear has now moved on quite far and dips towards the river
while straight above a waxing star seems set to grow for ever.
My courtyard? Candle now held high — two flames? That's not quite right.
Deep in the gorge, a monkey cries. A momentary fright.
Old white-hair, old but still quite hard!. I strut, I call, I warn:

I'm not a-bed; my staff's at 'Guard!'; who dares to chance his arm?

A Beauty Met by the Wayside
Li Bai

> White horse high-steps on fallen blooms
> knight's crop just brushes palanquin;
> pearls part to smiling concubine
> long nail suggesting
>
> > *That red house down there is mine.*

Springtime South of the River
Wei Zhuang

Men prattle of the pleasures of Jiangnan
say those that taste them never come home young.
In spring fine rains from azure sky
spot painted barques where lovers lie.
In cellars where each vintage charms
soft moons paint frost on bar-maids' arms.

Don't think it easy to depart
– to come back here will break your heart.

Clearly as ever I recall Jiangnan,
my youth, the meagre trappings of my spring:
slant bridge, a-horse, where damsels call,
red sleeves adorning every wall;
green screens, gold door-knockers, timeless hours
nights drinking, culling scented flowers.

Could I but taste such joys again
not weak old age would drive me home.

Missing Concubine

Emperor Wu of Han
Liu Che 140-87BC

Within, no sweep of silken sleeves is heard.
Her marbled courts unswept, dust undisturbed.
Her chamber, empty, cold, now stands forlorn
door blocked by leaves up to the second bar.
In search of loved-one, eyes pained, unappeased,
I dare not look to doubting heart for ease.

A Palace Poem

Gu Kuang

In marble halls, half-heaven high, reed pitch-pipe
  tones resound.
Winds waft away gay serenades, laughter of maids at play
till from dark clefts, unlit by moon, clepsydras only
  sound.
Blinds scrolled: two smiling stars, unveiled, outshine
  the Milky Way

Cold Marble Steps

Li Bai

My marble steps gleam white, now wet with dew.
It's late; in perfumed silks one's chilled quite through.
Step down, let fall the pearl and crystal screen,
watch tinkling droplets mirror autumn moons.

Cithara Player
Li Duan

Caressed by slender hands in halls of polished jade,
gold-fretted instruments, the best that craft affords.
She hopes to catch his eye, who now adjudicates,
succeeding several times at cost of doubtful chords.

Affairs of State
Zhu Qingyu

A quiet garden, shielding gate;
two palace girls escape the throng.
They've much to say, some affair of state
but listening parrots strike them dumb.

Autumn Night at the Palace
Wang Wei

Lit by a scythe of jade, chilled by an autumn dew
she'll wear but gauzy silks, nothing that is not thin.
She'll ply her silver cheng, strumming the whole night
   through,
won't face her empty room, won't yet give up, go in.

Lady-in-Waiting

Zhang Hu

Forbidden ground. The moon tops palace gates
to catch soft eyes of chicks in heron's nest.
She leans from shadows; with jade hairpin snuffs
a flame that might consume some fluttering moths

A Palace Girl's Lament in Spring

Du Xunhe

Can I be wrong to deck myself for spring
to use reflecting bronze to see all's well?
If dressing to one's best will not avail
can some one tell me what a maid must do?

It's stifling here: tired birds won't stir to sing,
no flowering shrubs yield shade when suns climb high.
With friends in years now gone, by brooks afar
I'd tuck behind my ear
soft cotton rose hibiscus flowers.

Court Lady out of Favour
Wang Changling

Her broom her grounds to grace his golden hall;
her fan her pass to stroll within his grounds.
Her fairness now eclipsed by raven plumes
it seems a rival's darkness shades the sun.

Palace Plaint
Bai Juyi

She dabs at tears but sleep won't come.
It's late. Hall shut – last songs long sung.
Not old, just ruddy. Favours fewer,
lone perfumed couch now all too sure.

At a Summer Palace
Wang Jian

Once Kings' Resort, now garden claimed by weeds;
a few red roses, petals under threat.
Two score of white-haired ladies no one needs
discuss old days, a life-time out of date.

Peach Blossom Dream

Tao Yuanming AD365-427
An Arcadian Fantasy (extract)

We're well content. Man's heritage is husbanding the soil:
no need of homes till dusk brings rest when evening suns go down.
There's shade beneath white mulberries to temper suns at noon
and who'd know when to plant his beans if he just sat at home?

In spring our silkworm harvest yields us fine long silken yarn;
our autumn crops are ours to reap, no princes' tolls distrain.
Through bare and empty wastes we all have freedom of the way,
just cockerels and barking dogs to break the calm of day.

Our rituals are seemly-kept, new-fangled notions spurned;
our clothes are made as always was, no manufactures worn.
Young folk and children play and talk, and sing too if they please
while drifts of white-haired ancients move from friend to friend at ease.

Men count the numbers of wild shoots to judge how mild the year
or judge from wind-wracked bushes when the winter will draw near.
Though we lack written chronicles to calendar our days
four seasons here divide the year and guide us in our ways.

A Peasant's Lot

Li Shen

*Plant well in spring. From each small grain
autumn will coax a noble head.
From sea to sea farms fill the plain.
Could farmers die for want of bread?*

   Hacking with hoe, sun right above now,
   sweat pouring down to the root of each stalk.
   How few know that crops are the fruit of man's brow,
   every grain eaten a peasant's heartbreak.

Silkworker

Zhang Yu

Off to town, no hint of frowns.
Kerchief wet when she returns.

Much display of silken gowns
but not by those who raise silk worms.

Weavers and Spinners

Yuan Zhen

Silk workers land their share of busy spells.
Spread out three times, the worms mature in swarms,
silk goddess in them spinning magic charms.

This year the tax is levied in advance.

It's justified, to meet official wants:
last year new wars consumed existing stocks;
conscripted men, sore battles fought, use silk to bind
   their wounds,
commanders, honour-laden, sorely need new silken
   screens.

She'll do her best to get her weaving done.
Warp tangles.
   Frames are stiff.
      This silk won't weave!

Next door, a white haired man keeps two girls home
unmarried. Once they've married they'll be gone
and how would he survive when once they leave?

>   Spinning and crossing under the eaves
>   slender and delicate, treading on threads,
>   skilful, ingenious, a spider at work.
>   Creature unmatched, knows the secrets of sky,
>   how to anchor in air perfect webs of fine gauze.

Panning for Gold

Liu Yuxi

Strained sunlight seeks out sandbanks ringed by mist
where women crowd stream bends to pan for gold.
Fine ladies' trinkets, seals of lords and kings
are won at cost from sands beneath cold streams.

Freshwater Perch

Fan Zhongyan

By the river. Folks dawdle and drift,
many ready to buy a fine perch.
But who sees the boat, like a leaf,
soar and sink on the wave-heaving surge?

Awaiting the Call

From the Shijing Collection c. 600BC

A well-built boat of cypress wood
is wasted, drifting on the flood.
   Disturbed and sleepless, pained, I wait
   the call to tasks that match my state.
   What leisured walk, what wine refined
   enough to occupy keen mind?

Unlike a mirror, I can't smile
with equal light on grace and guile.
   I do not favour kith and kin,
   take bribes or seek for private gain.
   I don't choose comfort, make complaint,
   but think right thoughts, act with restraint.

Like bedrock, my resolve is sound
no pebble to be kicked around.
   When people try to hide away
   their faults it's right that they should pay.
   Comported as befits my place,
   I'll never need to fear disgrace.

In anguish I accept my fate;
deserving praise I'm offered hate.
   I'm plagued with undeserved distress:
   insulted much, ignored no less.
   In dreams I strive lest Empires fall
   and waking gird, yet hear no call.

Great rulers reign like constant suns
while courtiers wax and wane like moons.
    Our sun grows dim, sharp dealers thrive.
    My sorrow will not let me live.
    Were I a bird and free to fly
    I'd spread my wings and seek the sky.

Empire in Disorder

Cen Shen

I've always known our age was out of joint;
when young I'd no respect for school or books.
If only then I'd learned to draw a bow
right now I'd head out east and fight the Huns.

I remonstrate, challenge official plans:
'You've made mistakes, should speed to put things right'
    Emperors can't be wrong. All's quite correct.
'A humble task will do, for one true man.'
    Swords comfort hands but only for a day.
    Your poems will stir men's hearts, point them the Way.
    Your duty's done, there's nothing more to say.

My mirror grieves, at grizzled beard and hair.
I'm patriot still, will be so all life long,
not bold – just don't have much I cannot spare.

Anxious Evening on the River

Du Fu

The faintest breath will sway tall grass by riversides
or towering masts of boats on lonely nights, half-seen.
A shooting star may fall from lordship over plains,
can't moons be veiled in cloud or drowned in surging
   streams?

What hope for one now ill, Court duties too severe?
What chance renown may come from writings, by and
   by?
Unknown, unheeded now, identity unclear,
lame gull ensnared in sand, despairing of sea or sky.

Returning to my Southern Hills

Meng Haoran

No gatehouse now holds my petitions back.
I'll home to dingy shack in southern hills.
   A prince must needs discard where talents lack
   – acquaintances can't woo one prone to ills.

Each year brings more white hair, speeds on again
as seasons rush to drive years to their close.
I'd cherish sleep. I'm gripped by aching pain.
Cold moons, dark pines my outlook in repose.

Zhongnan Retreat
Wang Wei

Mid-life I'd settled on The Way,
home nestling now beneath this hill.
Alone, I wander many a day –
   what's found alone gives added thrill.
I seek the source of streams on heaths
I sit and watch while clouds take birth
I'll meet a hermit in a wood –
   talking, laughing, happy then
     not giving thought to where or when
     or whether we should meet again.

Autumn Evening in the Mountains
Wang Wei

Late showers have cleared the hill. Why shun what shines?

This autumn eve the air's like spring, new-given:
a rising moon sheds light upon damp pines
while rocks and brook glow brighter now than heaven.
That fisherman just parting lotus leaves;
those washer-women jostling through bamboos,
do they not sense the spring in autumn's breeze?

Could autumn scents tempt me now from repose?

Finding My Place in Life
Bai Juyi

I hover, pick at food –
   my wine tastes dead,
   the flutes and strings
   no longer please my ear.
   My guests are in fine fettle,
   bondsmen fed –
the courtier's function blindingly laid bare.

To Magistrate Zhang
Wang Wei

In later life one's solace lies in peace,
don't strain your brain unriddling nature's ploys.
Don't plan for future life, that just brings grief,
much better to recall forgotten joys.

Let winds blow fragrant pine scents through your
   clothes,
make music in the moonlight. No one needs
to trouble over final truths. Who knows? –
don't anglers' songs find paths through trackless reeds?

Dwelling by a Stream

Liu Zongyuan

Long circumscribed by Mandarin belt
I'm happy to be exiled here,
afoot in neighbours' fields and plots
or living rough in wood, on hill.
At dawn I plough through dewy grass,
at dusk brooks chatter over stones.
One doesn't meet a single soul,
can sing all day beneath blue skies.

To Four Comrades in Exile

Liu Zongyuan

From my cell on this city wall wilderness crowds my
    view
boundless as sea or sky, stirring my fears anew.
Typhoons quite unforeseen swept court, hibiscus pool,
nailing, with driving hail, figs to the palace wall.

Uncounted leagues between – ridge, wood and
    fastness;
entrail-like, countless streams – gut-wrenching
    vastness.
Exile and fall from grace keep us now far apart,
far south where tattooed face glistens with patterned art.

Yet letters still ring true. We remain, as we were
comrades in thought and mind.
We share, we're proud to share
exile – still unsubdued.

New Year's Eve

Gao Shi

Inn lamps burn cold; who'd sleep alone?
Does every traveller freeze at heart?
My thoughts tonight far off, back home,
bring cares, grey hairs. So years depart.

Arriving Late at a Fisherman's Shack

Zhang Ji

A dingy hut where stream meets lake.
Old spray begrimes the flimsy door.

Not over-keen to share the floor
a traveller waits. Will the owner come?
Guest House? Too far, through thick bamboos.
The moon is out but boats are few.

There, by that shoal. Is that him coming into view?
that straw cape flapping in the breeze.

Inscription on a knife

from the Shijing Collection c. 600BC

Reveal me but don't seek strife
and I may save your life

Nightstop at a Village Inn
Jia Dao

The pillow's just a stone dredged from the brook
while water spurts all night from dripping wells
to fill a pool half hidden by bamboos.
Well seasoned traveller might be excused
for lying half the night quite wide awake
and listening to the storms up in the hills,
just waiting for the rain to catch him here.

Dawn Departure from Mount Shang
Wen Tingyun

Bells clang. At dawn mules budge.
Footprints in frost on bridge
dreams slip from travellers' clutch
cocks crow; moon silvers thatch
oak leaves strew roads from hills
orange buds hug tavern walls.
Wild geese wheel round this pond.

My dreams dart far beyond.

In Reply to a Poem from Magistrate Lu
Du Shenyan

A duty tour in early spring

Who but some courtier on a duty tour
too much afraid of all that's strange and new
may view, at dawn, pink clouds rise from the sea
count plum and willow mirrored in spring streams
share gentle airs with golden orioles
watch duckweed change its hue, touched by the sun,
only to think with longing of his home
stabbed by some snatch of half-remembered song?

East, West? Home's Best
Yuan Zhen

Far fields enthral: so much to view
from paths, new roads, Imperial Ways.
A thousand routes invite but who
would travel in his latter days?

I've had my fill of travel's pains.
I've stopped. Let's hope pain disappears.
No heart to plough through muddy plains
I'll hoard my strength and live for years.

Mission beyond the Frontier
Wang Wei

No other wheels but mine have marked these sands so far
in tributary realms where our ways are not known.
Exiled from Dragon Throne I fly, Ambassador,
wild goose in steady haste beneath barbarian skies.
All's desert, save where smoke soars up from lonely homes.
A yellow river tries to quench each setting sun.
At Desolation Pass, a cavalry patrol:
from Swallow Mountain now we exercise control.

Our Ambassadors Fail
Gao Shi

Men mill round, groups form up; whole armies take shape.
Tai horses seek ease in the chill autumn breeze.
Hardened Commanders stride, armour untied.
Young royals parade in their fur-lined brocade.

Lances at trail sport a wild panther's tail;
a pennant, blood red, flaunts a wolf's bleeding head.
The sun, going down, silhouettes the Tien Shan.

Bugles sound. *No reprieve.* Our ambassadors grieve.

Defending the Frontier

Du Fu

String bows taut if you'd keep tight frontiers,
our long arrows can wing from afar.
Kill their horses if tribes should appear,
seize their leaders, no need for real war.

To invade, slaughter tribes, is that good?
To transgress country bounds is insane.
Could we spill just Barbarian blood?
If we take barren lands, is that gain?

Facing the Snow

Du Fu

Just tears when battles make so many ghosts?
In sad old age I'll still recount the cost.
At sundown urgent clouds, lost where to go,
confused in crosswinds loose their loads of snow.

Who lacks for ladles when jars hold no wine?
Who'd beg hot embers when his firewood's gone?
No murmur in from any district round.
My task? Wake aching voids with anguished sounds?

Post Horse Relay

Yuan Zhen

An islet, Relay Post for Horse,
at first light bathed in heavenly glow.
Dawn breezes stir beasts in their stalls;
they munch, at ease, with bobbing heads.
The beacon guard enjoys his rest.

From River Pass, no sound of war:
no lines of battle needed here –
where flight's but four fleet feet away.

By the Restless River

Chen Tao

They swore to kill their foes at any cost.
Five thousand fur-lined cloaks now choke red streams.
Have pity on these restless bones now lost,
on wives who still embrace these men in dreams.

From a Belvedere

Li Bai

Kin fall like yellow leaves.
White faced, she gazes down.
Thin clouds above; blue seas,
cold colours. Autumn's come.

Hun soldiers crowd the sands.
They'll take him through Jade Pass
their 'guest'. When he returns
he'll find her, old, at last.

Geshu Han Defeats the Tibetans

Gao Shi

Springs flow, soiled with the blood of many clans.
Winds blow, to hound dead souls in spectral bonds.
Heads fly, ten thousand lances bear their weight.

In crowds, bound prisoners face the yamen gate.
Will evening's sallow dust see their ghosts weep
affronting heaven's pale twilight overhead?

Lament for Chentao

Du Fu

Ten counties' leading sons, unmourned,
all mud and blood, short lives adjourned,
    lie far as marsh extends.

Wide plain, clear sky, no noise of wars
yet forty thousand volunteers
    have this day met their ends.

Still cleaning arrows, Tartar hordes
fill market squares with uncouth words
    and drink and sing with friends.

Kin look north to Chentao through tears.
They see no sons and, sick with fears
    they know what that portends.

Drinking Song of Liangzhou

Wang Han

At ease, with precious grape in lucent cup
till summoned to take horse by clarion call.
No joke to rest on cold dry sand.
Drink up!
Of those who go to war, how many fall?

Evening Moon

Du Fu

Do you tonight in far Fuzhou
from your poor chamber see this moon?
I know you'll guard our children, dear,
too young to know wars keep me here.

The scented mist will damp your hair;
the moon's pure light will chill your arm.
Could I but come to keep you warm
bright moons would dry the tears we share.

To My Four Brothers Afar

Bai Juyi

Our years of labour brought to naught, our family home destroyed.
What help but from fast horses, what hope for us but flee?
No shelter left to shield us, ripe for pike and lance:
five brothers, now five exiles, determined to stay free.

We know now how wild geese must feel, sundered from their kin.
We're blown like rootless tumbleweed, scattered, sad at heart.
We share the sight of one same moon, make common cause in tears,
five brothers longing for one home, now homeless, far apart.

Guarding the Frontier
Lu Lun

A wild goose in the pale moonlight
the Tartar Lord has fled by night;

Light Cavalry, white sword and bow,
waiting to pounce, gathering snow.

The Weaver
Li Bai

Yellow clouds oppress the city;
rooks retreat to tree-high homes
cawing, screeching, croaking harshly,
drowning out the clack of looms.

At one, a woman from Qin River
weaves brocades and rarely rests.
Through her woven window screen
of gauzy yarn, soft emerald green,
she hears and stops ; the shuttle held.

Despair lays hold of her whole world.
Her thoughts fly far to war-torn men.

Tears gush – sharper than summer's rain.

Thinking of my Brothers
Du Fu

A martial drum. The wise stay home.
A wild goose calls.
Once autumn's come
these frontier dews soon turn to frost
with moons as bright as in winters past.

I don't know where my brothers are
nor where to ask if they're alive.
What hope a letter might arrive
when once again we're back at war?

Captive in Spring
Du Fu

Our State in ruin, yet streams and hills remain.
Now overgrown, rank weeds and shrubs reclaim
our city. Unlooked-for flowers bring tears;
hearts lurch as unexpected bird-song cheers.

The beacon fires have burned these three months
   gone.
I'd pay a ransome just for news of home.
My hair is now so white and scratched so thin
there's no bulk left to grip the wretched pin.

Awaiting News from Jade Gate Pass
Li Bai

Autumn
Chang'an. Now lit by moon
yet women wash and pound:
    from every door that single sound
    is carried on the dying autumn wind.

Their men face lawless hordes.
In every woman's mind one single thought
    Will mine return or not
    from Jade Gate Pass?

Winter
They force knives, needles, threads
– hands stiff and white with cold –
to stitch the fleeces they can hardly hold,
warm linings for their husbands' clothes.

Tomorrow at first light the couriers go.

Whose clothes will find whose man
before the long dark can?

Drifting at White Dragon Cave

Chang Jian

In evening light blue hills reveal new depths.
A lingering ray illumines Dragon Cave
and makes me dream of legendary lands
as we, afloat, buds mirrored in soft swell
drift west to merge unseen against the sky.
Away, far south, tall fleecy cumulous towers.

My mind recalls: Light streaks against brown moss
once seen as hair-bright tresses in deep shade
washed by a morning sun; Steep gushing springs,
wistaria trails, reflected on calm seas;
White cranes against far pines.
These waters stir old thoughts, make old hearts glow.

My flesh, once firm and young, no longer so;
indeed my bones feel brittle, old dried wood
but yet I strive, still longing to be one
with all I see, though fearful to intrude.
At times one needs to harbour thoughts alone.
Friends safe within the heart, what need of words?

We drift; I grasp at all that's to be seen
this silent evening, heart quite overfull.
Still calm, although so much eludes my grasp,
my spirit glories in these lapping waves.

At Poshan Monastery
Chang Jian

In the clear of the dawn this old temple entreats.
Here, unseen, the sun gilds the tops of the trees
to reveal winding paths guarding secret retreats
where flower-studded foliage is all the eye sees.

Light on the hillside stirs birds to take wing;
lakes, still in night, drown dark thoughts troubling
   men.
From the far world no sounds at all come –
only silence resounds amid stillness like stone.

On Mount Langya
Wei Yingwu

Mount Stonegate under snow, no trace of feet.
Damp drifts of mist now sharpen scents of pine
and heady incense lingering in the vale.
Today his courtyard pine-trees sport bright rags
where shivering birds hop down to glean their crumbs,
their Buddhist monk returned to welcome rest.

Wayfaring Songs of a Wandering Monk

*Extracts from the 'Song of Experiencing the Dao'
attributed to Xuan Jue, AD665-713*

XI
Defamed and slandered? What's blame or shame?
Sins torch high Heaven? I see no flame.
I quaff now this impure world, nectar to me
buoyed in unthinkingness, totally free.

XIV
Pilgrim to every sea, great river and lone hill
I've sought out sages' truths in quest of all life means,
what it might mean to die. A Master said, 'Be still'.
Now I in stillness see that life and death are dreams.

XXIII
Reflecting truths of which no detail fades
pure hearts secrete what's once observed in shell
to hoard ten thousand scenes in hallowed glades
securely treasured, layered in lucent pearl.

XXVIII (in part)
Still waters mirror many moons:
each moon regards One Moon above.
One Buddha-Spirit shines on men:
the radiant reflect that love.

Yi Gong's Meditation Chamber
Meng Haoran

Yi Gong raised meditation to high art,
contriving simple chamber by lone wood.

Beyond his door, a single gracious peak;
close by his porch, a tangle of ravines.
Until dusk falls, to hide faint prints of rain
blue skies are all the shade that touch his court.

He read the secret of the lotus flower
and knew to let no stain besmirch his heart.

Dedicated to the Hermit Cui
Qian Qi

Your path, that red moss carpet fringed with herbs;
your Physic Garden topped by mountain heights;
I envy all – your wine, your flowers, cool nights,
your dreams no fluttering butterfly disturbs.

For the Mountain Hermit of Quanjiao
Wei Yingwu

Winds cold as sin within the Prefect's walls.
How they must hound that hermit in his hills,
scouring ravines, gleaning sparse sheaves of thorns
to boil poor roots scarce better than white stones.

I hope that when I toast him here in wine
it comforts him on nights of wind and rain,
knowing we'd never meet on empty hills
where falling leaves obscure all trace of man.

In Search of the Daoist Monk Chang
Liu Changqing

Along The Way new worlds are met;
soft moss keeps track of sandalled feet.
Cloud-cumbered peak? We see chaste isle;
as gate, what some think weed-clogged stile.

Rains past, green pines feign richer hue.
Long slope traversed, Source springs to view.
Inspired as Buddha by a flower
we bow, his monks. Words have no power.

Translator's Note
Scrutinising the Inscrutable

Chinese traditional poetry provides a key to the supposedly inscrutable world of Old Cathay. However, early Chinese is economical of words and Chinese poets exquisitely economical in their choice of them. The poets say little explicitly but insist that it is not enough to read what is written on the lines. We are constantly invited to read what lies implicitly between the lines.

The poets present to us, in very few words, a set of building blocks yielding concepts, images, persons, places, actions, ideas, and meanings. But they provide few conjunctions, pronouns, tenses, or other grammatical indicators to suggest how these might be assembled. That is for us to decide. In Chinese each poem is a do-it-yourself package. Chinese readers know that poems may be read in many ways, and take delight in discovering new ways they had not previously noticed.

For Chinese reader or western translator it's a bit like buying a flatpack item of furniture from a store then trying to assemble it at home under the guidance of a deliberately inadequate set of instructions. One person may use the materials to make a bookcase and another to make a rack for pots and pans. Given reasonable luck, each may be satisfied with the outcome.

In one case only, the poem opposite, I have offered three different renderings to indicate a range of possible readings that might be inferred from one four-line Chinese text. However, I have judged that readers of this collection will expect me to have made a single finished poem in each case out of the building blocks provided by the Chinese poet, even if several other readings may be possible. That I have tried to do.

Can we in the modern west ever hope to fathom the wonders of Old Cathay? I believe that we can. And were the poets of Imperial China hoping to speak to later ages of the world? I believe that they were. Chen Zi'ang, AD 661-700, certainly tried. That we can read in English thirteen hundred years later, with understanding, the aspirations in this poem From The Heights of Youzhou, is a measure of his success.

From the Heights of Youzhou

Chen Zi'ang
(Three versions)[1]

I
Fathom minds of men of old
bequeath our wit on unborn age
mine heaven and earth of all they hold?
Frustrated tears denote the sage.

II
How to commune with souls long dead
to mould the mind of sage unborn
grasp time and space in one small head?
Thought sunders. Thinkers weep, forlorn.

III
Look back ten generations? How?
Look forward? Who knows what's in store?
Skies never end; time's evermore.
Each weeps. For what? He'll never know.

---

[1] For this poem only, three versions are offered. For the reasoning behind this decision see the Translator's Note opposite, 'Scrutinising the Inscrutable'.